YOU CHOOSE
BOOKS

FOUNDING THE
UNITED STATES

THE COLONISTS REVOLT

An Interactive American Revolution Adventure

by Matt Doeden

Consultant:
Richard Bell, PhD
Associate Professor of History
University of Maryland, College Park

CAPSTONE PRESS
a capstone imprint

You Choose Books are published by Capstone Press,
1710 Roe Crest Drive, North Mankato, Minnesota 56003
www.mycapstone.com

Library of Congress Cataloging-in-Publication Data
Library of Congress Cataloging-in-Publication data is available on the Library of
Congress website.

978-1-5435-1542-8 (library binding)
978-1-5435-1549-7 (paperback)

Editorial Credits
Adrian Vigliano, editor; Bobbie Nuytten, designer;
Kelly Garvin, media researcher; Kathy McColley, production specialist

Photo Credits
Alamy: Gado Images, 42, IanDagnall Computing, 89, Niday Picture Library,
62, PRISMA ARCHIVO, 39, Timewatch Images, 84, World History Archive,
97; Getty Images: Archive Photos/Stringer, 21, Bettmann, 28, Stock Montage/
Contributor, 33; North Wind Picture Archives, cover, 6, 10, 16, 48, 56, 64, 72, 78,
87, 103; Shutterstock: Everett Historical, 100, Stocksnapper, 67

Artistic elements: Shutterstock: Abstractor, photka

Printed and bound in Canada.
PA020

Table of Contents

ABOUT YOUR ADVENTURE

YOU are living in a time of change. The people of the North American colonies, under the rule of Great Britain, are growing restless. Talk of revolution is in the air. Will you take up the fight or watch from the shadows?

In this book you'll explore how the choices people made meant the difference between life and death. The events you'll experience happened to real people.

Chapter One sets the scene. Then you choose which path to read. Follow the directions at the bottom of each page. The choices you make will change your outcome. After you finish your path, go back and read the others for new perspectives and more adventures.

YOU CHOOSE the path
you take through history.

King George III ruled Great Britain from 1760 until his death in 1820.

THE SEEDS OF DISCONTENT

The streets bustle with activity. The clip-clop of horseshoes on cobblestone echoes off the city's stone buildings. The buzz of voices hangs in the air. The sky is clear and the sun is shining. Yet somehow it feels as though a dark cloud hangs over the American colonies.

An elderly couple walks by as you go about your daily errands. You can't help but overhear their conversation. "King George's taxes cannot be tolerated," says the man loudly.

"Lower your voice," scolds the woman, her gaze darting from side to side. "You never know when the British might be nearby. And their sympathizers are everywhere."

Turn the page.

"I don't care who hears me," the old man replies. "The colonies have put up with too much already. They want to tax us yet offer us no representation in Parliament? It's intolerable."

Their voices fade as they turn a corner. It seems that politics is all anyone wants to talk about these days. Even at home, it's the first subject discussed. Your brother goes on about defying the British while your father begs him not to do anything foolish. The colonists are divided. Many colonists remain loyal to King George III, but an increasing number of people seem to be talking about revolution.

You're not sure what to believe. Of course, you don't like having no say in how things run. And Great Britain is half a world away. What does King George know about the lives and challenges of his subjects here in the colonies? By what right does he rule here?

Yet revolt seems extreme. Revolt means open war with the most powerful empire in the world. Even if the colonies somehow managed to win such a war, the price in lives would be devastating. Part of you finds such talk to be terribly dangerous.

You shake your head, deep in thought. The colonies seem to be racing toward rebellion. Everything the British do angers them more. What will come next? What will be the final straw that finally turns talk into action?

9

To witness the Boston Massacre, a conflict between colonists and British soldiers, turn to page 11.

To attack the *Gaspee*, a British tax-collecting ship off the coast of Rhode Island, turn to page 43.

To take part in the taxation revolt known as the Boston Tea Party, turn to page 65.

British troops began occupying
Boston in September 1768.

CHAPTER 2

THE BOSTON MASSACRE

King Street is busier than usual today. It's March 5, 1770. You walk along the street on an errand for your mother with your best friend, Frederick, at your side. As usual, Frederick is going on and on, talking about anything that pops into his mind. At the moment he's going on about the western frontier. He says he'll blaze his own trail west to the Pacific one day.

You just smile and nod. You and Frederick have been friends for years, and he always has some fantastic future plan in mind. You know that in a day or a week he'll be on to some other big idea.

11

Turn the page.

As he explains his plans to cross the Mississippi River, Frederick suddenly trails off. "What is going on up there?" he asks. You raise an eyebrow. You hadn't noticed before, but Frederick is right. Something is happening. The sounds of voices—many people shouting—rise from the street ahead of you.

"I have no idea," you answer, taking a few steps forward. "Let's go find out."

You continue along King Street until you reach the source of the voices. A crowd has gathered outside the Custom House—a center for British taxation. The people surround a young man dressed in the red uniform of the British army.

"Go back to Britain, you pig!" shouts a man.

"Tell King George to come collect his taxes himself!" yells another.

Frederick looks at you with excitement. "It's a protest," he says. "Come on, let's join it."

You scan the crowd as it closes in around the young soldier. It's made up mostly of young men, and their shouting and taunting has a disturbing edge to it. This feels like more than a protest. It feels like trouble is brewing.

Frederick is already hurrying toward the crowd. It's just like him. He doesn't stop to think about what is happening or what might happen. He just sees something exciting and wants to be a part of it.

13

To join Frederick in the protest, turn to page 14.

To try to pull him away from the scene, turn to page 16.

Anti-British feelings are at an all-time high in the colonies, and Boston is at the heart of it. Perhaps it's time you stop observing and start taking part. With a deep breath, you square your shoulders and stride toward the angry mob.

"Go back to Britain!" Frederick shouts with glee. He seems to think this is great fun. But the other men in the crowd are not here for fun. That much is instantly clear.

A young man steps forward. You recognize him. It's Edward Garrick. The young man, who works for a local wig maker, is only a few years older than you.

"You never paid your bill!" Garrick shouts at the officer. He steps toward the officer.

The British soldier panics. He lunges forward, slamming Garrick in the head with his gun. You gasp as Garrick goes down in a heap.

The mob roars, its anger growing. The men close in on the soldier, who backs himself up against a doorway. His face shows a look of pure panic. Angry men begin throwing things at the soldier, who raises his gun.

Nearby church bells ring. That's usually a warning signal that there's a fire. But this is no fire. As people stream out of their houses, the streets fill with angry colonists.

"Look! There's more coming!" shouts Frederick. He's right. More red-coated British soldiers are hurrying to the scene, their guns at the ready.

To join in the shouting, turn to page 18.

To hang back, watching from the rear of the mob, turn to page 26.

"Hold on," you shout, grabbing Frederick by the shoulder.

"What?" he asks with a bit of anger creeping into his voice. "What's the problem?"

Disagreements between colonists and British soldiers became common in Boston during the British occupation.

16

"Look at that mob." You point at the crowd, which is growing by the minute and slowly closing in around the red-coated soldier. The roar of the mob grows as people shout insults at the young man. "They're pushing too far. Something bad is going to happen here."

Frederick pulls his arm away. "Stop it. This is a legal protest. The British aren't going to shoot at the king's own subjects! Now, are you coming with me or not?"

Frederick turns and begins to march toward the mob. Your stomach churns as you decide what to do. This feels very, very wrong.

To let Frederick go while you watch from afar, turn to page 22.

To use force to hold Frederick back, turn to page 24.

You elbow your way into the crowd, raising your fist and shouting, "Down with King George!" Before you know it, you're nearly at the front of the mob.

The British soldiers fight through the crowd to come to the aid of the trapped soldier. You hear Frederick grunt as he's shoved out of the way. He falls over, lost in the mass of people.

Part of you realizes that the situation is spiraling out of control. But you find yourself swept up in the moment, and seeing your friend shoved only fuels your anger. You and the rest of the mob continue to press in toward the trapped British soldier. What can the other British soldiers do? You can't imagine that they would fire at civilians on a busy street.

"Everyone, please go home!" shouts a British officer. But the mob doesn't go home. Instead they block the street, cornering the British. The Redcoats raise their guns, pointing them straight into the mob.

Just then a man to your left steps forward. He hurls a club at the soldiers. The weapon strikes one of the Redcoats in the head. The soldier goes down to the ground. As he stands up, a crack of gunfire rips through the evening air. The sound echoes off the stone streets.

Suddenly the street erupts in chaos. Another British soldier fires his gun into the crowd. All around you people are screaming, yelling, and crying. Another shot rings out. Then another.

To dive for the ground, turn to page 20.

To run, turn to page 28.

There's nowhere to run. The street is packed with people and they stand behind you like a wall. In their panic the British have started shooting into the crowd, and you're in the line of fire. So, you do the only thing you can—you throw yourself to the ground.

In the chaos you're kicked and trampled. Shots continue to ring out, and a dark-skinned man next to you falls down dead in a heap. With horror you realize it's Crispus Attucks, a dockworker you've met several times. As the chaos continues you cover your head, trying to protect yourself until it is all over.

The British have stopped shooting. The young officer, whose face is ghastly white, orders the crowd to disperse. Several men lie groaning in the street. You're battered and bruised but otherwise unharmed. And you have a powerful urge to get out of here.

Crispus Attucks

You scan the mob, searching for Frederick. There's no sign of him.

"Everyone, back to your homes!" repeats the officer. "Now!"

To leave, turn to page 30.

To continue searching for Frederick, turn to page 32.

You can only watch as your friend disappears into the growing mob. You stand back, watching as the situation grows more intense. Every now and then you catch a glimpse of him, but as more people join in, you lose him.

The shouting and taunting soon turn to violence. People in the mob start throwing objects at the young Redcoat, who appears to grow more nervous. The man slams the back of his weapon into one protester. The man falls in a heap as the mob gasps.

"Look out!" you shout, as you see more Redcoats rushing to the scene, their guns at the ready. One of the soldiers begs the mob to break up and the people to return home. But the mob drowns out his pleas.

Then, in an instant, everything changes. Someone throws a club at one of the Redcoats.

The soldier goes down. As he scrambles to his feet, his gun fires into the air.

The shot was an accident. But the other Redcoats don't know that. They hear the shot and respond by shooting into the crowd, cutting down one civilian after another.

The street erupts into chaos. The sounds of gunfire fade and are replaced with shouting, screaming, and sobbing. "Get out of here!" shouts an old man as he rushes past you, fleeing from the scene.

23

To search for Frederick, turn to page 32.

To flee, turn to page 35.

A feeling of dread hangs over you as you look at the shouting mob. These people are angry and they're only making themselves angrier with their yelling. You just don't see any way that this ends well, and you can't let Frederick get swept up in it.

You lunge forward, wrapping your arms around your friend. He squirms and shouts at you as you pull him back. "What are you doing?" he screams. "Let me go! Have you gone mad?"

Frederick spins out of your grasp. He wheels around to face you. His jaw is clenched and his eyes are narrow. You've never seen him this angry.

"Get off me," he hisses at you. Frederick turns and starts back toward the mob.

Again you grab him. This time you tackle him to the ground. But Frederick is lightning quick. In a heartbeat he's over you, fists flying.

You try to roll away from him but he's stronger than you realized.

Suddenly a shot rings out. In an instant your fight is over. You both brush yourselves off and rise.

"The Redcoats!" Frederick says, his voice cracking, "They're shooting at the colonists!"

To rush toward the mob to help, turn to page 37.

To run away from the gunfire, turn to page 39.

This is getting out of hand. You turn, spotting Frederick nearby. "We have to go!" you shout over the noise of the mob.

Frederick looks at you as though you are crazy. "Go? Are you joking? I'm not leaving!"

With that, he turns and disappears deeper into the mob. The chants and jeers seem to be growing louder by the second. A quick glance at the gathering British soldiers tells you that the tension is growing rapidly. You're certain that violence is at hand, and you don't want to be anywhere near it.

You make your way out of the mob and briskly walk away. You're a block away when the first gunshot rings out. You quicken your pace. Another shot rings out . . . then another . . . and another. The sound of gunfire gives way to screaming and shouting.

Your walk turns into a run. It sounds like a massacre back there, and you want no part of it. You don't know it at the time, but the incident playing out behind you will change the course of history. You could have seen it firsthand. Of course, you could also have been among the dead. Perhaps running was the wisest decision.

THE END

To follow another path, turn to page 9.
To read the conclusion, turn to page 101.

As the sounds of gunfire ring in your ears, you panic. You turn to run back, away from the scene. But behind you stands a mass of people, most of whom are in a similar panic. You try to push your way through the crowd, but you just can't seem to get through.

There were about 4,000 British troops in Boston at the time of the Boston Massacre.

CRACK! Another blast rips through the air. Suddenly you feel a sharp pain and a strong force pushing you back, away from the British. For a brief moment, you imagine that someone is trying to help you.

But soon you realize the truth. You put your hand to your belly and it comes back red. You've been shot. You stand there for a moment before the strength in your legs fails. You can hear screaming as you slump to the ground.

The last thing you see is Frederick's face. He can't save you. But at least you can die knowing that he's all right. Five people are killed in the event that becomes known as the Boston Massacre. Unfortunately, you're one of them.

THE END
To follow another path, turn to page 9.
To read the conclusion, turn to page 101.

You stumble away from the scene. People are lying on the ground, moaning. Others are motionless and appear to be dead. You can barely understand what has happened and how close you came to being among the dead and wounded.

You feel like your head is in a fog. Over and over in your mind, you see the image of the man right next to you going down. You make your way home. Your mother gasps at the sight of you. In short, stammering sentences you manage to explain to her what just happened.

The news about Frederick comes several hours later. You overhear as the young man who lives next door explains it to your father. "I'm sorry," says the young man. "He was shot. The surgeon said that he would have survived with immediate care. But no one helped him until it was too late. I'm sorry, but Frederick passed away."

The words echo through your head. *Gone? Without so much as a goodbye?* You think back to that moment right after the attack. Should you have looked for your friend? Would it have made any difference? You know it's a question you'll never stop asking yourself.

THE END

To follow another path, turn to page 9.
To read the conclusion, turn to page 101.

"Frederick!" you shout, scanning the crowd. A man in a dark jacket lies on the street, bleeding from a wound to his shoulder. Another lies motionless nearby. Your stomach turns as you realize that the man is dead. You're struck by fear that you'll find Frederick the same way.

For several minutes you make your way through the scene, searching. Finally, you spot Frederick. He's lying in the street, near the Common House. He looks back at you with glassy eyes, then points to his upper leg. "I'm shot," he says with a voice barely higher than a whisper. His trousers are soaked in blood.

You don't hesitate. You scoop up your friend and carry him away. "We need a doctor!" you shout. It doesn't take long before a doctor finds you. You lay Frederick down on the street while the doctor rips open Frederick's trouser leg.

Five colonists were killed by British troops during the Boston Massacre.

"We need to stop the bleeding," says the doctor. He hands you a handkerchief. "Here, hold this tight against the wound." Frederick shouts in pain as you press against the wound. The doctor removes his belt and ties it around Frederick's leg, cinching it tight. The bleeding slows and eventually stops.

Turn the page.

"Your friend will need more treatment," says the doctor. "But he should survive, thanks to your quick action. Well done."

You feel no pride as you look down at Frederick, who has passed out from the pain. What happened here today? Could it have been avoided? You wonder what it will mean for the future.

Those are all questions for another day. For now all you care about is making sure Frederick is all right.

THE END

To follow another path, turn to page 9.
To read the conclusion, turn to page 101.

The man is right. The violence may not be over and there's no telling how the British will react. You turn and hurry away from the scene, ducking down a side street. The screaming fades in the distance.

A woman stops you. "What happened?" she gasps. "I heard gunshots!"

"The British," you stammer. "They opened fire! They shot at the crowd!"

The woman's face grows pale. You grab her arm, fearing that she might faint. After a moment she shakes her head. "No, don't worry about me. I'm all right. I have to go help. If people are hurt, I can help. Will you come with me?"

Turn the page.

You shake your head. Your decision is made. Witnessing the Boston Massacre was more than you could handle. You'll let others lead the fight for independence. You don't plan to ever put yourself in harm's way again.

THE END

To follow another path, turn to page 9.
To read the conclusion, turn to page 101.

You can hardly believe your eyes. A handful of British troops are firing directly into the crowd of protesters. Another shot rings out. People begin panicking as they try to get away from the gunfire.

While others run away, you and Frederick rush toward the chaos. A man lies on the ground, clutching a wound. Maybe you can help!

You hurry to the man's side. But before you can get there, more shots ring out. You feel a sharp pain and a powerful force knocks you right off your feet. For a moment you wonder who knocked you down. But as you put a hand to your shoulder, it comes away red and wet.

"Oh no," Frederick gasps, kneeling by your side. "You're shot."

It's true. In your rush to help, you ran right into the line of fire.

Turn the page.

"Doctor!" Frederick shouts. "We need a doctor!"

Frederick presses his hand on the wound as you wait for help. You're losing blood and growing light-headed, but his quick thinking has slowed the blood loss.

"Don't worry," Frederick says. "Help is on the way. You're going to survive this and you're going to be a hero!"

You smile. You like the sound of that. You close your eyes and wait. Help will come soon.

38

THE END

To follow another path, turn to page 9.
To read the conclusion, turn to page 101.

"We have to go!" you shout. You turn and
hurry away, half dragging the stunned Frederick
behind you. As you weave through the streets,
more gunfire echoes off the stone buildings.

The Boston Massacre helped unite more
colonists against Great Britain.

Turn the page.

You don't stop running until you're far away. Finally, you both collapse, gasping for breath.

"I'm sorry," you huff. "Frederick, I truly am sorry. I just knew that something bad was going to happen. I . . . I had to get us both out of there."

Frederick gives you a long look. After a few moments, he shakes his head and shrugs. "I just want to go home. Let's go."

The news of the shooting sweeps through Boston like wildfire. You recount what you saw time and again—to family, friends, and neighbors. You even tell your tale to a young silversmith named Paul Revere. Revere seems intensely interested in every detail of what becomes known as the Boston Massacre.

"This is only the beginning," Revere tells you. "Revolution is close at hand. Be ready for it."

You know he's right. You shake his hand and nod your head. "I will be. We all will."

THE END

To follow another path, turn to page 9.
To read the conclusion, turn to page 101.

Abraham Whipple led the first naval attack on British forces in the American Revolution.

CHAPTER 3

THE GASPEE AFFAIR

Abraham Whipple looks at you with a gleam in his eye. A cool dawn breeze blows across your small boat as it pushes off from the wharf. A small crowd of your fellow Rhode Island colonists has gathered there, and they're buzzing with excitement.

"Are you ready for this?" Whipple asks as you both dip oars into the water and begin to row.

You nod. You heard the news early this morning. The hated *Gaspee*, a British ship charged with regulating trade in Rhode Island, had run aground and a group of colonists are planning to destroy it. You knew right away that you wanted to take part.

Turn the page.

"I am, Captain," you reply, with more confidence than you feel. Now that you're actually on your way to destroy the ship, you begin to grasp how big this really is. After all, the plan is to set fire to a British ship. The British won't take that sort of thing lightly. You're afraid to imagine what sort of response it will bring.

Whipple slaps you on the back and smiles. Your boat, along with several others, cuts across the water in near silence as dawn lights the sky. Soon the *Gaspee* is within sight. The ship is grounded on a sandbar. Its captain is waiting for high tide to move it back to deeper waters. But for the moment, it is stuck.

"There she is," whispers Edmund, one of your neighbors. He sits across from you, rowing. To be honest, you and Edmund have never really gotten along. He's a crude and cruel young man.

But here, now, on this boat, you feel a certain bond with Edmund. You're in this together, for good or bad.

Edmund gives you a crooked smile. Actually, you realize, it's more of a snarl. "I hope the Brits burn along with their ship," he sneers. Suddenly that bond you felt disappears. You can only shake your head. You're here to destroy a ship, not burn sailors.

Whipple stands as you approach. "Who comes there?" calls a voice from the ship.

"I want to come aboard!" Whipple shouts.

After a brief pause, the answer comes back. "Stand off. You can't come aboard."

Whipple smiles. He knew what the answer would be.

Turn the page.

"I have come for the commander of this vessel," he shouts, his voice carrying over the still water. "I will have him, dead or alive!"

Whipple turns toward you. "Men, spring to your oars!"

Just like that it begins. The boats swarm the grounded ship. As you surge forward, you spot a rope dangling from the *Gaspee*. Your path is taking you directly toward it.

To remain on the boat, go to page 47.

To grab the rope and start climbing onto the *Gaspee*, turn to page 48.

All around you colonists are boarding the *Gaspee*. With their ship run aground, the British are helpless to defend themselves. You remain until you're the last man on your boat, craning your neck to watch what is happening above you.

You will your body to move. But it doesn't seem to respond. Your hands tremble and your legs feel weak from the terror at what might go wrong. *What am I doing out here?* you wonder. Above, from the *Gaspee*'s main deck, you can hear the hooting and hollering of the men. Above the din of voices you hear shouts of "Burn it! Burn it!"

You shake your head. Something big is happening and here you sit. It's not too late to join in.

To climb aboard, turn to page 48.

To remain here, safely away from the action, turn to page 61.

From the moment you haul yourself up the rigging rope, everything happens in a blur. The deck of the *Gaspee* is in chaos as the colonists swarm the ship. The British resist at first, but they are overwhelmed by the number of colonists.

When the Revolutionary War began, the colonists had no organized navy. By 1775 patriot leaders had formed the Continental Navy.

Several of the colonists—including Edmund—are determined to kill the British. But others quickly squash that idea.

"Bind their hands!" booms a voice. You recognize the speaker, Dr. John Mawney. "Do not harm the sailors."

No sooner do the words come out of his mouth than you hear the blast of a musket below decks.

"That came from the cargo hold!" Edmund shouts. "That's where the fighting is!"

To go below decks to the cargo hold, turn to page 50.

To remain on the main deck, turn to page 52.

You charge below decks, where an eerie silence replaces the shouting. You pull up as you see what has happened. A British sailor lies on the deck, bleeding heavily from a wound high on his left leg. Behind you someone whispers, "It's Lieutenant Duddingston!"

Suddenly your legs go weak. Until now this has seemed like an adventure. Now, suddenly, a man's life is at stake. What are you doing here? Why did you come? You wish you could take it all back.

Dr. Mawney is close behind you. The doctor springs into action, placing his hands on top of the wound. "We must stop the bleeding," he says. "Someone help me!"

To retreat above decks and let someone else help,
go to page 51.

To step forward to help the doctor,
turn to page 54.

50

The sight of blood makes you feel dizzy. Your stomach churns and your legs go weak. Another man whom you do not recognize steps forward to help the doctor. The man holds his hands over the wound as Dr. Mawney works on Duddingston. Within moments the man's hands are stained red with blood. The sight makes you retch.

You know you have to get away from the blood. Without a moment's hesitation, you turn around and charge back up to the main deck.

Turn to page 52.

Above decks the colonists are busy binding the British sailors' hands. Some of the men taunt the British. "You won't be taking any more taxes from us," one hisses. "Let King George come for his taxes himself," boasts another. "We'll give him a Rhode Island welcome!"

As the minutes tick by, you and the other colonists feel a growing sense of unease. "This is taking too long," Edmund says. "Why haven't we torched this ship yet?"

"There's a wounded Redcoat below decks," calls out another voice. "They're tending to him."

Meanwhile, the eastern sky grows brighter and brighter with every passing minute. The men grow restless. Finally, the order comes. "They're ready! Let's burn this ship!"

It all happens very quickly. The *Gaspee* erupts into flames as you and the colonists flee the ship.

You help march the British prisoners off the ship, then climb onto a boat yourself. As you move, one of the British scowls at you. "You will all pay for this, and dearly. I will remember your face. When you return to shore, I suggest you run and never come back."

The words leave you with an empty feeling in the pit of your stomach. Is he right? Will the British seek revenge?

To flee in order to avoid punishment, turn to page 57.

To go home and take your chances, turn to page 59.

Before you even have time to think, you step forward. You kneel down next to the British sailor, Duddingston. "Place your hands here," says Dr. Mawney, pointing to the wound. "Give it firm pressure."

"There are linens in that chest," Duddingston says, his voice filled with pain. Dr. Mawney orders another man to fetch the linens and tear them into strips.

You can feel Duddingston's pulse beneath your hands, which are soaked red with blood.

"Mawney!" shouts a voice from the door. "We have to go! Let's set this fire and get out!"

"Not yet," the doctor barks back. He is focused on his patient. The call comes again, but the doctor refuses to move.

The doctor works quickly, fashioning a bandage. On his order you lift your hands and he swiftly places the bandage on the wound.

"All right," he finally calls to the men. "Light the fire."

Dr. Mawney turns to you. "Get this man above decks. We have little time. Go!"

Duddingston groans as you help him to his feet. You support his weight as you climb above decks. As carefully as you can, you help to lower the injured man onto a boat. All around you the colonists are fleeing the *Gaspee*. "She's aflame!" shouts Edmund. "We've done it!"

You join the others. As quickly as you arrived, you flee. As you row away from the grounded ship, you watch as fire engulfs it. The ship goes up like a torch, the flames climbing into the early light of dawn.

Turn the page.

About 50 colonists participated in the attack on the Gaspee.

Duddingston gives you a long, cold look. "You fools don't know what you've done," he says, his voice weak.

You can only nod your head. He's right. You've started something here today, and there's no telling where it will lead. One thing is for sure. You'll never forget your brief, chaotic moments aboard the *Gaspee*. And the British won't forget them either.

THE END

To follow another path, turn to page 9.
To read the conclusion, turn to page 101.

56

By the time you return home, you're panicking. You just helped destroy a British ship. What will the British do? Will you be arrested? Imprisoned? Or worse?

No matter how hard you try, you cannot shake the feeling of dread. You're convinced that Redcoats will break down your door at any moment. So you do the only thing you can do. You pack a few things, bid farewell to your friends and family, and take to the road.

It's a hard life, away from home. You eventually make your way to Philadelphia, where you work for a cobbler. One day in the cobbler's shop, you overhear some men talking about the burning of the *Gaspee*.

"What happened to the men who burned it?" you ask.

Turn the page.

"Nothing!" booms one of the men. He bursts out laughing. "The British didn't do a thing. Didn't arrest a single man. They're weak, you see. And that's why we must declare our independence and be rid of them once and for all."

You shake your head. Is it true? Was no one punished? Did you leave your home for nothing? Or was the man just boasting?

You've begun to make a life here in Philadelphia. But you decide it's time to head home to Rhode Island. War is coming, and you want to be with your family when it arrives.

58

THE END
To follow another path, turn to page 9.
To read the conclusion, turn to page 101.

You head straight home once you return to land. Your hands shake and your mind races. But in the end, you decide not to run. This is your home. Where else would you go?

In the days that follow, the burning of the *Gaspee* is the talk of the colony. The British question colonists, but no one gives away your identity—or that of any of the colonists who took part. Days turn into weeks, weeks into months. Word of what you've done spreads through the colonies, where it is celebrated.

The feeling of unrest has hung over the colonies for years. But now it has changed. More often colonists are openly calling for revolution. They want to be free from British rule, and the burning of the *Gaspee* marks a major victory and a turning point.

Turn the page.

"War is coming," Edmund tells you one day. "I'm going to be there to fight. We beat the British once. We can do it again."

You nod. He's right. War is coming. And you will do your part to fight. But the British are strong and resourceful. They won't give up their colonies easily. Dark days lie ahead. Will they be worth it?

You'll all find out together.

THE END

To follow another path, turn to page 9.
To read the conclusion, turn to page 101.

Just a few minutes ago, you were filled with courage and excitement at the idea of setting fire to a British ship. But now the reality of it has you paralyzed with fear. No matter how hard you try, you just can't bring yourself to board the ship.

What were you thinking, coming out here? You're not made for this sort of adventure. You should have just stayed home, safe and sound.

From the water you listen and watch as your fellow colonists set fire to the *Gaspee*. Soon they begin fleeing to the boats, dragging the British sailors along with them as prisoners. One of the Redcoats is shot, but it appears that he will survive. None of the colonists were harmed.

As Edmund climbs aboard, he gives you a look of disgust and shakes his head. You pretend not to notice.

61

Turn the page.

The destruction of the **Gaspee** was a powerful symbol of colonial resistance to British rule.

You row away as flames engulf the *Gaspee*. The men hoot in celebration. They seem to share a unique bond from the experience, and you feel left out.

Once you're back on land, you march home. That's where you'll stay. And when revolution does come, you'll remain at home. Others can fight the war. You have no place in it.

THE END

To follow another path, turn to page 9.
To read the conclusion, turn to page 101.

Small group meetings in cities around the colonies provided important places for revolutionary ideas to grow.

CHAPTER 4

THE BOSTON TEA PARTY

"Go get your brother," you mumble to yourself as you make your way along Boston's bustling Milk Street. "Bring your brother home. Help your brother."

Lately it seems as though your parents spend most of their time worrying about your brother, John. Ever since he joined Samuel Adams' patriot movement, he has been a constant worry for them. And when John is off doing whatever revolutionaries do, it always falls to you to go and fetch him.

Not long ago John was much like you are. You're frustrated with how the British are governing the colonies. Taxes are a burden.

Turn the page.

And you're interested in hearing about the growing independence movement. But those problems are bigger than you are. You'd rather focus on day-to-day life and leave those sorts of troubles to other people.

As you weave through the crowds of people in the chilly December air, you look up. Before you stands the Old South Meeting Hall. The church is the biggest building in Boston, and it towers over the city. The street grows more packed as you approach the building. People are buzzing about the meeting being held inside. "Adams is speaking!" you hear one woman say. Colonists file into the church by the thousands. John is in there, somewhere, and you're supposed to make sure he stays out of trouble.

As you enter the hall, a voice booms over the gathered crowd. The place is packed. Every pew, aisle, and gallery is filled with people.

Everyone in the hall is focused on the speaker, Samuel Adams. He speaks about the Tea Act, a wildly unpopular British tax on the colonies.

Samuel Adams began arguing for colonial independence from Great Britain in 1748 in his newspaper, The Independent Advertiser.

Turn the page.

According to the law, the tax to the British is owed as soon as tea is unloaded from a ship. Right now, in Boston Harbor, ships carrying British tea are anchored. Today is the day that Governor Hutchinson has ordered the tea to be unloaded—an act Adams wishes to forbid.

You scan the hall, finally spotting John in a pew not far from where Adams stands. You weave your way through the crowd until you reach him. "John," you whisper, grabbing him by the shoulder. "Come on. Let's go."

John scowls. He grabs your arm and pulls you down next to him. "Shhh," he says. "Just sit and listen."

With a sigh you settle in. At first, Adams and the other speakers say little to sway you. But the longer you listen, the more you start to agree with them.

"No taxation without representation!"
comes the argument, time after time. Soon you
find yourself repeating it back, along with the
gathered crowd. The British, the speakers insist,
have no right to tax the colonists, who have no
representation in British Parliament. It seems
like a valid point.

The people wait eagerly for news of
Hutchinson's decision. Finally, the big moment
comes. A report comes back that, one last time,
the governor has refused to send the tea back
to Britain. Adams stands and declares, "This
meeting can do nothing further to save the
country."

The crowd roars. John wears a wide smile.

"What's happening?" you ask him.

69

Turn the page.

"It's the signal," John explains. "We're going to go to Boston Harbor to dump the tea into the ocean."

Already men are filing out of the hall. John stands to follow them. He turns back. "Well," he asks. "Are you going to join us?"

To join in dumping the tea, go to page 71.

To refuse, turn to page 74.

You find yourself swept up in the moment. It must be the enthusiasm of the speakers and the excitement of the crowd. Everything is a blur as you're whisked toward one of the doors that leads out of the hall.

Outside, dozens of men are pulling on Mohawk Indian–style headdresses. They are disguising their faces with paint. John presses one of the headdresses into your arms. "Put this on," he says.

For a moment you just stand there, staring. "This isn't going to fool anyone," you protest.

John smiles as he puts on his headdress. "It's not supposed to fool them. It's a message. We are Americans, not British," he says. "Plus it does give us a bit of a disguise. I'm not worried about how the British will respond, but there's no point in making ourselves easy to identify. Come on!"

Turn the page.

Printed posters called handbills were an important form of communication among colonists. In 1773 handbills warned patriots against buying British tea.

The group, dressed in disguises, dashes through the streets, the men hooting excitedly. You join in, caught up in the moment. "To Griffin's Wharf!" you shout.

"Let's see how tea mingles with salt water," John replies.

Once at the wharf, the group breaks into three groups. You and John follow your group's commander onto one of the ships. The ship's captain greets you.

"Give us the keys to the cargo hatches," your commander demands.

The captain offers no resistance. He hands over the keys. "Do as you will," he says. "But please do not damage my ship."

Your commander agrees. You're here for the tea, not to destroy ships.

"Break into teams!" orders your commander. "We need men opening crates while others dump the tea!"

To open crates, turn to page 79.

To dump tea, turn to page 81.

You shake your head in disbelief. The patriot independence movement has some good ideas. But dumping tea into a harbor—what will that prove? It seems foolish and wasteful, and you won't be a part of it.

John shrugs. "Have it your way," he says, turning and disappearing into the mass of men moving toward the doors. You can only watch as they leave the hall, donning feathers and headdresses designed to make them look like American Indians.

The crowd files out, hooting and hollering, until only a few remain in the hall. As you look around, you're surprised to find Adams not more than a dozen feet from you. He speaks with other leaders of the patriot movement but notices you watching him.

"You're not joining the party?" he asks.

You shake your head. "It's not for me," you answer. "But . . . why aren't you going? Wasn't this all your idea?"

Adams takes a few steps and places his hand on your shoulder. "I would love nothing more than to be there," he says. "However, the leaders of our great movement—myself, John Hancock over there, and others—simply cannot be seen there. It would give the British cause to arrest us, which they would certainly do."

"I see."

"Tell me," Adams continues, "what do you think of our movement? Do you disagree with what we're trying to accomplish? Do you not want freedom from Britain?"

Turn the page.

You think for a moment. "I do," you decide. "What you said here tonight made sense. I'm just not sure that dumping tea into the harbor will really change anything."

Adams smiles. "Go to the harbor. Watch what happens there. You might change your mind." He pats you on the back, then turns to speak with the other leaders of the movement.

You slowly make your way out of the hall. You can still hear the roar of the crowd as the marchers make their way toward the harbor.

To go and watch at the harbor, go to page 77.

To go home, turn to page 89.

Perhaps Adams is right. You may not be willing to participate in this protest, but you'd be a fool not to at least witness the event. You make your way along Milk Street to Griffin's Wharf, where the three ships carrying the controversial tea are anchored. Already the group of men, including John, has split into three groups and boarded the ships. The men are dressed as Mohawk Indians, complete with headdresses and tomahawks.

"My goodness," says a woman nearby. "They aren't really going to throw all of that perfectly good tea into the water, are they? What a waste!"

"It's not a waste," replies an old man. "It's a statement, loud and clear, for King George. The colonies are ready to stand on their own."

The disguised men are busy cracking open crates and dumping the contents into the water.

Turn the page.

In 1774 tea-dumping protests spread to other colonies such as New York and South Carolina.

Not far from you, a large pile of tea has spilled onto the wharf. You stare at it. It's worth a fortune. You could probably grab a bit of it for yourself without anyone noticing.

To grab some tea, turn to page 86.

To continue watching, turn to page 91.

You and John get to work, using small hatchets to pry open the first crate of tea. As the crate cracks open, the pungent smell of tea is almost overwhelming. You've never been much of a tea drinker, but your mother loves it and it smells wonderful.

The two of you haul the crate to your fellow disguised colonists, who pitch it overboard. You can't help but laugh as it spills into the sea, the great mass of it slowly sinking.

And so it goes. It feels like a party on the ship as you open and dump crate after crate. And all the while, you breathe in the delicious aroma of tea. As you work you can't help but think about what your mother would think of this and how much she would love to have some of this tea for herself.

Turn the page.

In a quiet moment, you find yourself alone in a cargo hold. You glance down at your jacket, lined with pockets. Would it hurt to grab just a handful or two for her? No one would ever know the difference.

To continue opening crates, turn to page 83.

To take some tea, turn to page 93.

Every job is important, but you want to be one of the protesters who dumps the tea into Boston Harbor. You and John work together. Once your fellow protesters crack open the first crate, the two of you hoist it to the railing of the ship.

John gives you a big grin. "Here we go," he says. All eyes are on you.

With a surge you push the crate over the rail. It tumbles down into the dark water below, its valuable contents spilling into the sea. All around you the men cheer. The crowd that has grown to watch you echoes the cheer. You feel like you're about to burst with pride.

Over the next few hours, you continue dumping tea at a brisk pace. The work leaves you feeling tired. That feeling soon turns into pure exhaustion. Your arms and back ache.

Turn the page.

Suddenly, you feel light-headed. John grabs you by the arm.

"Slow down," he says. "Are you okay? You're not looking so well."

You don't want to stop. So far there has been no response from the British. But you want to finish this task and get out as quickly as you can.

To take a break, turn to page 84.

To tell John that you're fine, turn to page 97.

"No," you mumble to yourself. This isn't about you. It's about something much bigger. You believe that your actions today are noble. Taking this tea for yourself would be stealing. After a few moments, John returns and you resume your task.

After a few hours, you crack open the final crate of tea. Above decks the excitement remains high. Your men dump the last of the tea, happily singing and patting each other on the backs.

"Time to go," John says. "It is done. We have to leave."

Turn to page 95.

You sit down on the deck. Your head swims.

"Just rest for a minute," John says. "You've exhausted yourself."

Protesters dumped an estimated 92,000 pounds of tea into Boston Harbor.

He's right. Your hands are shaking and you feel dizzy. You relax for a few moments, taking deep breaths and recovering your strength. Soon your hands steady. The feeling of dizziness passes. You stand up and get back to work, careful to pace yourself.

Finally, the moment comes. You and John dump the final crate of tea into the ocean. A cheer rises throughout the ship. It's done! Your fellow protesters pat you on the back and congratulate each other. At that moment you feel tremendous pride in yourself and your colony.

"The party is over," shouts your commander. "Everyone, go home!"

Turn to page 95.

Perhaps both the woman and the old man are right. It may be a message, but it's also a waste. Maybe . . . just maybe . . . you could grab a bit of tea for yourself and no one would notice.

Trying not to draw attention to yourself, you make your way to the tea. With a quick glance around, you begin to line your pockets with the precious leaves. Handful by handful you fill every pocket in your jacket. You're just about to slink away when a voice rings out. "Hey! He's taking the tea!"

Immediately, all eyes turn to you. From one of the nearby ships, even the men unloading the tea stop for a moment to look at you with disgust. You feel small and ashamed, and you fear John might be one of the men watching.

"Get him!" shout several of the colonists.

Many of the protesters brought hatchets or small axes as tools to assist with destroying the tea.

In a panic you take off, running as fast as your feet will carry you. But you've drawn too much attention to yourself. A young man catches you, tackling you to the ground. The gathering crowd jeers at you as the men pull the tea from your pockets.

Turn the page.

"Traitor!" they shout. "Turncoat!"

The men strip you of your jacket. They drag you back to the wharf. And then, in the greatest moment of humiliation in your life, they throw you into the frigid water of the harbor. A cheer goes up as everyone points and laughs. You cannot hide your shame as you pull yourself from the water and rush home.

You hope no one recognized you. But you know better. It's a shame you'll carry with you the rest of your days.

88

THE END

To follow another path, turn to page 9.
To read the conclusion, turn to page 101.

You have no desire to watch what John and the others have planned. What if it all goes wrong? What if the British take action to stop it? And even if they don't, what's the point of it all?

Historians estimate that hundreds of people took part in the Boston Tea Party.

89

Turn the page.

Shaking your head, you make your way back home. John returns hours later. At first your parents are concerned. But as he tells them how his group dumped tea into the harbor, both of them smile. Soon they're all laughing and calling for freedom from the British.

You watch from the corner, sulking. Perhaps you missed the chance to be a part of something important today. Maybe your careful nature left you out of something big, something that will be remembered throughout history. Missing out on the Boston Tea Party may be something you regret for the rest of your life.

THE END

To follow another path, turn to page 9.
To read the conclusion, turn to page 101.

You shake your head, laughing at yourself for having such a thought. Here before you is perhaps the greatest protest against the British that the colonies have ever seen. Yet you were thinking about taking some tea? Nonsense!

You watch over the next few hours as crate after crate of tea is cracked open and dumped into the water. You imagine the water, already dark and murky, growing brown from all the tea. The ever-growing crowd cheers with every crate that is dumped. John and the men on the ships make a great show of their work.

By the time it's over, you can't help but feel a great sense of pride in what your fellow colonists have done. You make your way home. You're eager to tell everyone you know about what you saw and that your brother played a big role in it.

Turn the page.

You regret not taking part in the protest. But you're glad that you were there to see it happen. You got a chance to see history unfold, and you'll never forget it.

THE END

To follow another path, turn to page 9.
To read the conclusion, turn to page 101.

"Oh, why not," you tell yourself, scooping up a handful of the precious tea and stuffing it into one of your coat pockets.

"What are you doing?" John shouts. You freeze.

"I thought you were above decks," you stammer.

"You're stealing the tea?" John's voice quivers.

"Just a bit, for mother," you insist.

John's expression grows cold. "Go home," he says. "Leave the tea. We're here for something larger, for a cause. We are not petty thieves. That cheapens what we've done here tonight."

"I'll put it back," you plead. "I'm sorry . . ."

"GO!" John roars. From his tone you know there's no changing his mind. You empty your pocket and leave the ship, never turning back.

Turn the page.

News of the tea in Boston Harbor spreads throughout the colonies. It is celebrated as one of the greatest moments of the growing patriot movement. Yet you feel only shame about your part. John never mentions the incident. He acts as though you weren't even there. The gulf between the two of you had started to close when you joined him that night. But the moment he caught you stealing tea, that gulf grew wider.

When war breaks out with the British in 1775, John is among the first to sign up to fight. He is also among the first to die. The two of you never get a chance to repair the damage that was done to your relationship that night. And you'll regret it for the rest of your life.

THE END

To follow another path, turn to page 9.
To read the conclusion, turn to page 101.

You wake early the next morning. Your muscles ache from all the work of the evening before, but you don't mind.

"Come on," John shouts from the next room. "We still have work to do!"

You groan, pulling yourself out of bed. "What are you talking about?"

"The tea," John replies. "Huge masses of it are still floating in the harbor. I'm worried that the British could try to recover some of it. We can't let that happen."

And so your work continues. You and John take a small rowboat out into the harbor. In the cold morning air, you make your way from one floating island of tea to the next, using your oars to push the tea down into the water. Several other boats are busy with the same task.

Turn the page.

It doesn't take long. Soon there's not so much as a dry leaf to be found.

"What will happen next?" you ask John.

He shrugs. "I don't know. Maybe the British will respond. Maybe not. But one thing is certain. News of what we've done will spread up and down the colonies. We've taken a major step toward independence . . . and war. I think history will remember what we've done."

You can only hope he's right.

THE END
To follow another path, turn to page 9.
To read the conclusion, turn to page 101.

You wave John away. "Let's get this done before the British decide to do something about it."

And so it's back to work. You dump another crate and then another.

Most people who participated in the tea dumping kept their identities secret for years. Many of the protesters' names are still unknown.

97

Turn the page.

As you bend over to hoist the next crate, the world begins to fade. Black creeps in around the corners of your eyes. Your knees go weak.

You faint on the deck, striking your head on the railing. The next thing you know, several colonists—including John—stand over you.

"I'm fine," you insist. You try to get back on your feet, but your knees buckle once again.

"No, you're not fine," John argues. "You're bleeding."

He's right. You hit your head when you fell, and blood gushes from a gash in your forehead. "We have to get you home," John says, supporting you as you rise.

"No, no," you reply. "We've come so far. I don't want to go."

John just shakes his head. "We're going. Now."

With that, your part in the Boston Tea Party is over. You'll never forget the role you played, but you'll always regret not being able to see it through.

THE END

To follow another path, turn to page 9.
To read the conclusion, turn to page 101.

The Declaration of Independence was approved by the Second Continental Congress on July 4, 1776.

CHAPTER 5

MOVING TOWARD INDEPENDENCE

By the 1770s the relationship between Great Britain and its American colonies was in tatters. The British had invested a lot of resources in the colonies, especially in the fighting of the French and Indian War (1754–1763). They tried to regain some of that investment by taxing the colonists who benefited from it. The British passed a series of taxes, which were generally hated by the colonists.

Some colonists, called loyalists, still supported King George's rule over the colonies. But the voices of the patriot movement increasingly drowned them out. Patriot leaders such as Samuel Adams and John Hancock wanted the colonies to form their own nation.

A string of events, mainly in the early 1770s, pushed the colonies to the brink of revolution. In many ways the event that would become known as the Boston Massacre was a turning point.

During the incident, which happened on March 5, 1770, British troops shot into a mob of protesting colonists. They killed five and wounded others.

Patriot leader Paul Revere immortalized the scene in his engraving, "The Bloody Massacre in King-Street." Revere's artwork turned into a piece of patriot movement propaganda, fueling an ever-growing anti-British feeling among colonists.

Protests against British taxation grew more common. In some cases protest turned into action.

Georgii III. Regis.

C A P. XIX.

An Act to difcontinue, in fuch Manner, and for fuch Time as are therein mentioned, tho landing and difcharging, lading or fhipping, of Goods, Wares, and Merchandife, at the Town, and within the Harbour, of *Bofton*, in the Province of *Maffachufet's Bay*, in *North America*.

HEREAS Dangerous Commotions and Infurrections have been fomented and raifed in the Town of Bofton, in the Province of Maffachufet's Bay, in New England, by divers ill affected Perfons, to the Subverfion of His Majefty's Government, and to the utter Deftruction of the publick Peace, and good Order of the faid Town; in which Commotions and Infurrections certain valuable Cargoes of Teas, being the Property of the Eaft India Company, and on Board certain Veffels lying within the Bay or Harbour

The Boston Port Bill closed the Port of Boston and required that the people of Boston pay for the tea destroyed in 1773.

On June 9, 1772, a group of colonists burned the *Gaspee*. This British tax-collection ship had run aground in the coastal waters of Rhode Island. Colonists celebrated the destruction of the *Gaspee*, and the act emboldened the patriot movement.

The most famous anti-British protest, the Boston Tea Party, occurred on December 16, 1773. Colonists dressed as Mohawk Indians boarded three ships carrying British tea. They cracked open more than 300 crates of tea and dumped them into Boston Harbor. The British responded a year later, passing the Coercive Acts (which became better known to the colonists as the Intolerable Acts). They stripped the colony of Massachusetts of its right to self-government and shut down commerce in Boston. This only added to the tension in the colonies.

A year later the fighting in the Revolutionary War began. On July 4, 1776, the colonies officially declared their independence from Great Britain.

These three events were far from alone in sending the colonies down the path toward revolution. Yet all three were key in fueling the fire. They helped shape the history of the patriot movement and convinced the colonists to separate from Britain. What followed was a long and bloody war. But in the end, the colonies won their freedom and the United States took its place on the world stage.

TIMELINE

March 5, 1770—During a protest over taxation, British troops fire into a mob of protesters, killing five; the event, later known as the Boston Massacre, enrages colonists and fuels the growing patriot movement

June 9, 1772—A group of Rhode Island men board and then burn the British customs ship HMS *Gaspee*, which had run aground the night before

May 10, 1773—Great Britain's Parliament passes the Tea Act, sparking massive protests in the American colonies

December 16, 1773—When the colonial governor of Massachusetts refuses to send three shiploads of tea back to Britain, colonists dressed as Mohawk Indians board the ships anchored in Boston Harbor and dump the tea into the water

1774—The British Parliament passes a series of acts in response to the Boston Tea Party, collectively known by the colonists as the Intolerable Acts

April 1775—The fighting begins in the American Revolution in the Battles of Lexington and Concord

July 4, 1776—The colonies officially sign the Declaration of Independence, asserting their independence from Britain

September 3, 1783—The Treaty of Paris officially ends the American Revolution; Great Britain recognizes the independence of the United States of America

OTHER PATHS TO EXPLORE

In this book, you've seen how events from the past look different from three points of view. Perspectives on history are as varied as the people who lived it. Seeing history from many points of view is an important part of understanding it. Here are ideas for other Revolutionary War points of view to explore.

+ Leading up to the Boston Massacre, a mob of colonists surrounded a British soldier. The colonists shouted insults at the soldier and even threw things at him. Think about how he reacted. What would you have done in his place?

+ Some colonists remained loyal to Great Britain and King George III. What reasons might these loyalists have had for remaining loyal? Why didn't they join the patriot movement?

+ At the Boston Tea Party, British sailors aboard the ships that carried the tea offered no resistance to the colonists. Why not? Would you have fought to protect your ship's cargo?

READ MORE

Caravantes, Peggy. *The American Revolution: 12 Things to Know*. North Mankato, Minn.: 12-Story Library, 2017.

Stokes, Jonathan W. *The Thrifty Time Traveler's Guide to the American Revolution: A Handbook for Time Travelers*. New York: Viking, Penguin Group, 2018.

Yomtov, Nelson. *Night of Rebellion!: Nickolas Flux and the Boston Tea Party*. North Mankato, Minn.: Capstone Press, 2014.

INTERNET SITES

Use FactHound to find Internet sites related to this book.

Visit *www.facthound.com*

Just type in 9781543515428 and go.

GLOSSARY

chaos (KAY-os)—total confusion

colony (KAH-luh-nee)—a place that is settled by people from another country and is controlled by that country

headdress (HED-dress)—a decorative covering for the head

independence (in-di-PEN-duhnss)—freedom from the control of other people or things

intolerable (in-TOL-ur-uh-buhl)—something so harsh or bad that it cannot be accepted

loyalist (LOI-uh-list)—a colonist who was loyal to Great Britain during the Revolutionary War

massacre (MASS-uh-kuhr)—the needless killing of a group of helpless people

Parliament (PAR-luh-muhnt)—the national legislature of Great Britain

patriot (PAY-tree-uht)—a person who sided with the colonies during the Revolutionary War

propaganda (praw-puh-GAN-duh)—information spread to try to influence the thinking of people; often not completely true or fair

revenge (rih-VENJ)—an action taken to repay harm done

traitor (TRAY-tuhr)—someone who turns against his or her country

BIBLIOGRAPHY

Carp, Benjamin. *Defiance of the Patriots*. New Haven, Conn.: Yale University Press, 2010.

Hinderaker, Eric. *Boston's Massacre*. Cambridge, Mass.: The Belknap Press of Harvard University Press, 2017.

Raven, Rory. *Burning the Gaspee: Revolution in Rhode Island*. Charleston, S.C.: History Press, 2012.

Unger, Harlow G. *American Tempest: How the Boston Tea Party Sparked a Revolution*. Cambridge, Mass.: Da Capo Press, 2011.

Wood, Gordon S. *The American Revolution: A History*. New York: Modern Library, 2002.

INDEX